WordPress 4 Business Website Redesign With custom coding of imported database

Stephen Link

DEDICATION

I would like to give thanks to my God. Without Him, life would be unbearable. Thanks also to my wife who has supported me through the research and study time required to complete this book.

Thanks, also, to those who have been in my Publishing/Promoting classes. In trying to give back in the same proportion that I have received, it seems that just as much knowledge was gained, as was imparted, in these classes.

The opportunities to develop WordPress sites for my clients in order to promote their business interests are greatly appreciated. Along the way, I have received the knowledge and confidence to create this book. I wish you, the reader, a great adventure in your web site design/redesign efforts.

CONTENTS

ACKNOWLEDGMENTS

Acknowledgments go out to the many who have supported the WordPress web publishing platform and the numerous plugins available to enhance your web site. You are encouraged to support those hard working developers who will commit so much time to producing high quality plugins with functionality that helps to bring revenue into your business.

I would also like to give thanks to those dedicated hikers who provided the pictures used in the WalktheAT program. It is your strength and commitment that keeps the trail open for others to enjoy.

1 THE FIRST STEPS

Let's start at the beginning – registering a new domain name. You may have a preferred web host and know that the company will give you the best deal on domain registration and hosting. Then again, you may not be so certain of the deal that you have been offered. My experience with Godaddy has been great. In addition to the excellent service and support, I appreciate their economical pricing. I registered my new domain, ncwebdesignprogramming.com, with them and received a year of hosting, as of August 2014, for only $41.88. Yes, that is the price for one year including the domain name registration. To make this deal even better, it can be extended for up to three years at the same annual price.

Have you had experiences of spending hours on the phone and waiting days for a new domain to be active and available? Yes, I have experienced that also – years ago. Domain registration did not take an hour – it was closer to ten minutes, if even that long. During that ten minute period, I selected the $3.49 per month hosting account, searched and verified my domain name, submitted payment and received setup verification. Depending on your advanced preparation (and the efficiency of the selected web host), your time frame for these processes may vary.

SIDE TRIP Do some web browsing and compare the features and prices of various web hosts. You will find excellent deals such as that shown for GoDaddy above. You may even find a deal such as $1 per month. Always look at the "after" price of any deal that you encounter. For example, the $3.49 per month package with GoDaddy reverts to $6 or more per month after the special pricing expires.

In many cases, you can extend the deal up to five years. This, also, should be approached with caution. If you are starting up a new business, it may not be around for five years. On the positive side of that thought, it is always good to be optimistic.

Now we can cover another subject mentioned in the title – WordPress. Due to the ease of setting up a site, my currently chosen CMS (Content Management System) is WordPress. As of this writing, the latest version available is 4.1. Other than username, password and email address, all other options were left at default settings. The best part is that, using the GoDaddy "Installatron" Control Panel, you can have the base WordPress installation in place over the next 15 minutes.

On GoDaddy's CPanel, select WordPress from the Web Applications section. Provide a few details to be used in setting up your site and everything will be available in just a few minutes. Yes, it can be that easy!

If your host does not have a "Control Panel" based setup for WordPress, you will need to take the route of copying and extracting files before running the SETUP process for WordPress. Additionally, you will need to create the database to be used by your WordPress CMS. This process can be rather lengthy, but it is explained in detail on the WordPress site.

Have you kept track of the time? We should have less than a half hour into the process so far. With that minimal time invested, we have a new domain name registered and have a very basic site in place. Anyone who visits your new domain name will see the default WordPress template (shown below) instead of an "under construction" page. The default WordPress theme used in this screen shot is called "Twenty Fourteen."

Have you called a friend across the country or in another part of the world, and your new site cannot be viewed? This is not your fault, or your host's. It may take a few hours (up to 24) for updating the DNS (Domain Name Server) entries across all servers of the World Wide Web. This is expected, but complete replication will eventually happen. Depending on the size of your web host and DNS settings on your computer, it could take a few hours for you to access the new site. You can use a web site called "What's My DNS," which is located at https://www.whatsmydns.net/ to verify propagation of your domain name across the world's DNS servers.

A positive side effect of this time lag is that you have a few hours to improve the site before everyone will be able to view it. With WordPress, you can accomplish quite a bit in a few hours. Let's now sample and select a WordPress theme that works best for our specific purpose. This process could take hours of installing and activating new, free, themes or it could take a few minutes if you have already selected, and possibly paid for, the theme for your new site.

How many steps does it take to change your theme? If you are selecting from the WordPress themes available directly through your WP Control Panel - four.

Hover over Appearance and click Themes

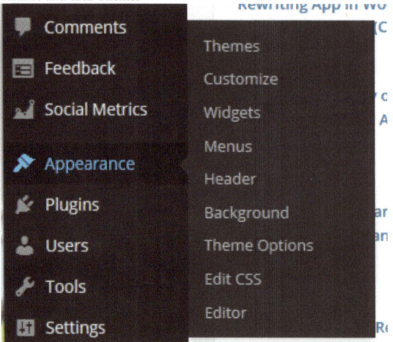

Click "Add New"
Select a theme and click the Install button
Activate the new theme

First, let's take a look at a rather unique blog site design called "Spun." You may like this theme because of the responsive nature and unique blog design. There are no pages shown here, other than a single blog page, although specific pages can be integrated with this theme. You can post links at the top of the page to outside pages, either your own or those of friends and advertisers. These are in the upper right of the page, but they are not shown in this screen shot.

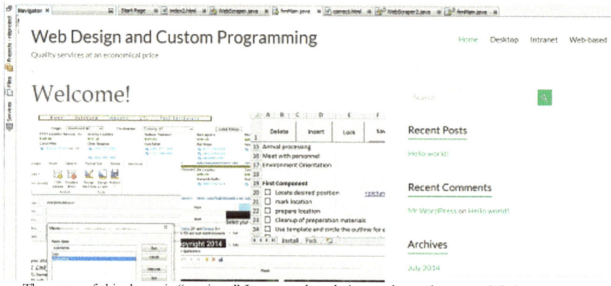

The name of this theme is "spacious." It was used to design my latest site – ncwebdesignprogramming. Notice the background picture selected. That is actually a composite of two screens selected from the NetBeans programming environment. This background is quite fitting for the focus of the site and the services offered - web site design and custom programming. The site has changed a little since this original design, but it is still based on the "spacious" theme.

Fourth Post

 Posted on Aug 11, 2014

This is the fourth post to be displayed and it si really long so that I can see if the Read More option will be displayed. If I could get rid of the bottom stuff, this would work well and probably receive the blessing of all involved

[MORE]

🗁 Posted in News

Post Number 3

Next we will look at a blog site that has been heavily customized to display only a few functions. The name of this theme is "Accesspress Lite." This is a site that functions merely as a messaging front-end before redirecting to a main web site. Functions such as featured section, sliders and social have been turned off to provide the minimized effect shown here.

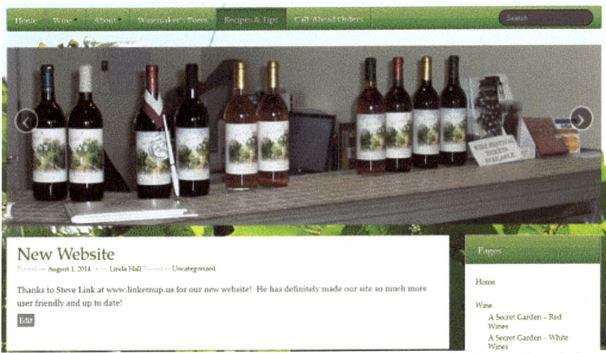

The final theme that we will illustrate is called "iFeature." Redesigning an older, but complete, site based on this theme was accomplished within an eight hour working day. The site was designed for a winery and the grape vines in the background picture fit beautifully. What you see in this screen shot is a "shout out" to LinkEmUp for designing their new web site, which is live, responsive and fully operational.

In this first chapter we have registered our domain and looked at a four of the free themes available for download and simple installation from within your WordPress Dashboard. Many more themes are available ranging in price from free to hundreds of dollars. For the right amount of money, you can even purchase unique ownership of a theme. After reading this Ebook, you may feel adventurous enough to modify a base theme and create your own custom theme from that.

Of course, you want a theme that fits well with your intended web site purpose. The color scheming and the graphics for the winery site shown above are a perfect example of proper theme selection. There are many web sites that are dedicated to creating free or low cost themes that offer select features seen in the premium productions. One of these sites can be found at www.web2feel.com. I have previously utilized their Marina theme because of the many options and customizable settings available. A few other third-party offerings that may be worth checking out are:

www.themeforest.net
www.wphub.com
www.1001freewpthemes.com

Keep in mind that you can switch between themes without any content loss. Let's say, for example, that you have a blog site with 200 blog posts. You want to switch the theme but are afraid of loss in content or functionality. You "bite the bullet" and make the switch after backing everything up. Voila, all posts are in place and the site looks beautiful since you did the research and selected a theme with perfectly matched color and design features.

SIDE TRIP It is time for a little more web browsing and decision making. Sit down at your computer, or with a piece of paper and pen, whichever fits your personality best. Answer the following questions, along with any additional criteria that you may think of.

Do you want a slider on your main page? Should that slider also be available on other pages?

How will you be integrating social networks with your web site? Will these be used for your own sharing purposes or to allow others to share your blogs with their network?

What approach will you take for exposure in the search engines? You can pay for advertising within the search engines and the social networks if the advertising budget allows.

How involved do you want to be in the programming side of customizing your web site? All WordPress sites are completely customizable in the area of fonts, colors, layouts, etc as long as you "get down and dirty" with the code and CSS that drives the site. Some, on the other hand, are customizable from within the dashboard. The advantage of the programming approach is that anything can be accomplished, given enough time and money. The disadvantage of the programming approach is that without a specific backup process, those changes can be lost if you change or update the selected theme.

All of these desired features can affect the theme that you select. Careful planning is necessary to ensure that the chosen theme fits your desires and is quite appealing to the general users. A much used term in the past few years is "User Experience," also known as UX. This broad term encompasses everything that involves the web site visitor from the navigation of the site to the user's opinion of each browsing session on your web site. Your goal in web design is a memorable and exciting user experience that not only keeps them coming back again and again, but is so memorable that your users tell others and invite them into the enjoyable experience.

2 GETTING INTO SITE DEVELOPMENT

We are in the process of a complete business web site redesign using WordPress. So far, we have selected our host, signed up for a hosting plan, registered the domain name, installed WordPress and selected a theme. The steps and processes covered in this chapter can be taken in any order desired.

For this example, we will be using the "spacious" theme. We are starting with the basic, unmodified, version. By the end of this chapter, we will be able to set up our pages, add and set up plugins, upload and utilize media plus other steps to be included in the early stages of setting up a site in WordPress. The starting design of the "spacious" theme is shown below.

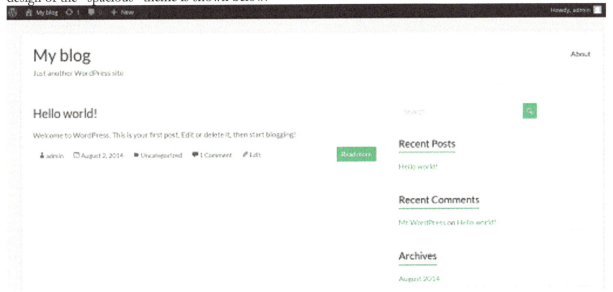

Are you impressed? I must admit that an empty theme in any CMS is quite plain and unimpressive. Let's get productive!

The first thing to do is add some plugins. One plugin that provides a large amount of functionality is called "Jetpack." Another highly useful plugin is called "WordPress SEO by Yoast." Although there are a huge number of useful plugins that fit specific needs, we will install and set up only two more in this chapter - "Wordfence Security" and "Captcha." You should install these by going to Dashboard-plugins-Add New, search by the name and "Install Now" for each. After installation, you will need to activate the plugin. Additionally, setup may be required for specific plugins. Go ahead, install and activate all four of the plugins now. You should keep in mind that a generic search such as "Captcha" will show many items (422 for this term in January 2015). Use the suggestions in the following **SIDE TRIP** to determine which specific plugin is desired.

SIDE TRIP We will install four plugins that provide some necessary functionality in the areas of security and search engine optimization. You should not cut your site, or users, short on functionality. As of April 2013, a general web search revealed that there are over 30,000 plugins available for installation. When installing plugins, you should be aware of many different factors, including the few listed below.

When is the last time that this plugin was updated?

How much feedback does it have and how does it rate?

Is it possible that this plugin will conflict with another that you have installed?

Is the functionality truly useful to you, as administrator, or your visitors?

Now that we have the plugins installed, let's set them up. We will start with what I consider to be the most important plugin available for WordPress – Jetpack. This plugin installs many different types of functionality. Some of these are mobile theme, contact form, socialization of your blogs and many more. First, connect Jetpack using your WordPress.com account. If you don't have one, registration is free.

Next, you may want to activate some of the features within Jetpack. Click on Settings and activate additional options and/or deactivate some that are enabled by default. Although not complete, I definitely recommend Spelling and Grammar, publicize (social postings) and mobile theme. A screenshot is shown below with many of these options listed. Those showing the vertical bar to the left of the name are active.

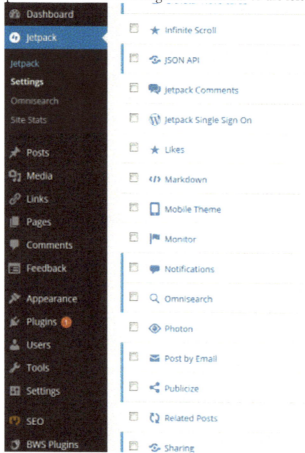

Let's move on to the next important functionality – search engine optimization. That functionality, in this case, is enabled by the "WordPress SEO" plugin and the settings can be accessed to control many settings and features. Select the SEO button, shown on the left side of the screenshot above. Clicking on that will open the many settings available. Since the SEO subject and implementation of search engine solutions can get very deep and consume entire books, setup of WordPress SEO will not be covered in depth, although you are heavily advised to learn as much as possible about search engines and use that information in setting up your WordPress SEO module.

The screenshot shown here regards the XML sitemap. This is an integral feature that allows proper indexing of your site by the search engines. Unless you want your site to be invisible to the rest of the world, this option should be checked (the default) and you may even want to check the other two search engines.

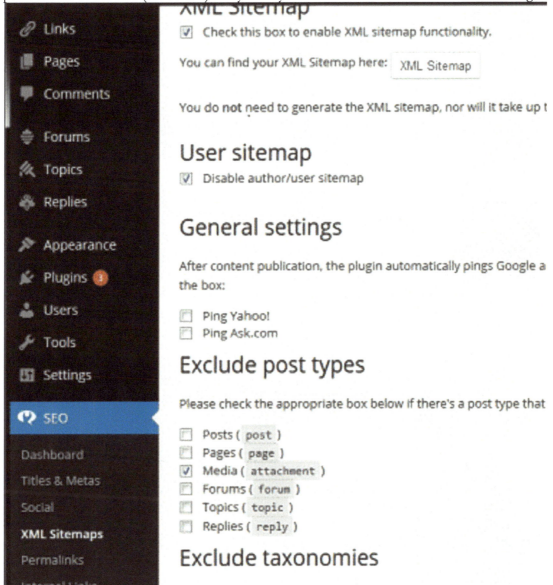

If you don't like the features available with this plugin, or believe there should be more or fewer setup options, select and install a different plugin. For most WordPress features, the number of plugins available number in the double or triple digits.

Next, let's cover a useful security feature – Captcha. If you have run a blog before, or have participated in discussions or form submissions, you have probably experienced the Captcha security feature. The basic functionality is to require a question to be answered to login, post, comment and even submit forms. This feature will help greatly in controlling the automated bots that want to use your blog to spread their spam.

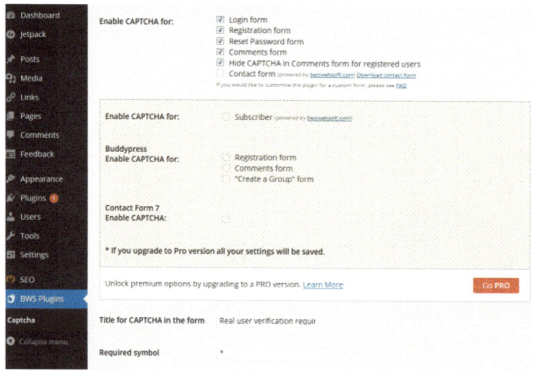

Notice the title typed in the field. I used "Real user verification required." Depending on the settings selected at the top of this screen, all activity on your site can be protected by Captcha.

Let's move on to the final, though definitely not least important, plugin covered in this chapter – Wordfence Security.

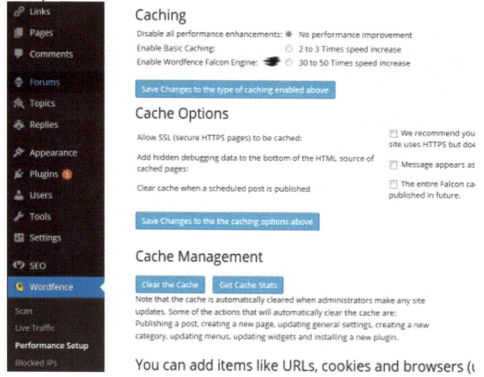

What you see in this screenshot is the basic, default, performance settings for Wordfence. Although these initial settings are quite adequate, they are not optimal. After working with your site for a few months, you should return to these settings and optimize the blocked IPs (based on attempts to log into your system with a failed admin password), cache settings and other adjustments.

NOTE We have installed four plugins, and you may have selected some others for installation and setup. You will occasionally, sometimes weekly or more often, receive a notification that updates are available for plugins. Use caution when applying these updates, because a failed update installation can leave your site in maintenance mode; inaccessible even to the administrator. I have experienced this quite a few times and it is generally tied to Jetpack updates.

One guaranteed approach for recovery is a full backup (I use the UpdraftPlus plugin) of your site before installing any updates. In an emergency situation, the first option to try is to disable all plugins through your database control panel and then re-enable them and apply updates again. Backing up is an excellent step to take prior to applying additional plugins, in case they should conflict with another and cause a problem. See Appendix A for detailed instructions for disabling plugins using GoDaddy and phpMyAdmin.

Why are updates such a necessity? The simplest answer to that is "the bad guys out there want your stuff." It seems that there is a new vulnerability announced every week regarding operating systems, content management systems, web hosting software and many other areas. A software update, once designed and tested, is the only way to make your "stuff" secure again. For example, it is now December of 2014 and there have been two version updates to WordPress in the past two months. The first was a major version update to 4.0 and there was recently an update to the 4.0.1 version and now 4.1 (January 2015). Without applying these updates, your site and visitor information can be hijacked and used for criminal purposes.

Now that we have the plugins installed and set up, let's move on to creating pages for our WordPress small business site. In the Dashboard menu, click on Pages and then Add New.

Add New Page

This is a test to be used as the home page

Permalink: http://www.ncwebdesignprogramming.com/testsite/this-is-a-test-...-the-home-page/ Edit View Page

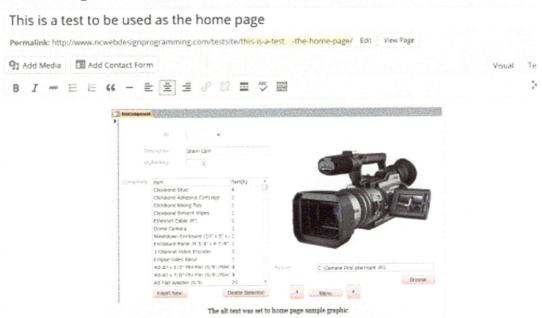

The alt text was set to home page sample graphic

This test page will be the home page shown when people browse to our web site. We used "Add Media" above and uploaded/inserted a graphic onto this page. We have also modified the permalink, graphic alt text and body text to score well in the SEO check.

div » dl » dd

Word count: 46

Draft saved at 4:15:34 pm

Notice the body text that we have typed and the graphic inserted using the Add Media button. Also notice the fact that we will be setting this as the default page for our site. When inserting a graphic, be sure to add appropriate alt text. This alternate text will help with search engine optimization of your post. Another reason for the alt text is to ensure ADA (Americans with Disabilities Act) compliance of your web site. For appearance purposes, you will be able to select different sizes of your image – be sure to select an image that fits well in your desired format. Later, we will set this as the home page, but that is accomplished outside of the page itself.

Now let's consider how the search engines, and the world, will discover our new web page. See below for an initial display of the "WordPress SEO" plugin.

This doesn't look so good, but we can fix that. Let's change the title to something more appropriate for the intended search term – "home page web site." Maybe "Setting up web site home page in wordpress" is a better title and "web site home page" is a better search term. Now we have a YES on both article heading and page title.

Two more easy changes are Page URL and Meta description. Click Edit near the top of your page beside of Permalink. This will allow changing of the URL used for the blog post. Change it to "web-site-home-page-in-wordpress" (being sure to use dashes instead of spaces). You will also enter these words, among others, in the Meta description box near the bottom of your page. How does it look now?

We have made quite a few changes and improved some in the focus keyword area, but the overall SEO ranking is still "Poor." We can start at the top and fix just a few reported issues to greatly affect our ranking. Since this test article will not have 300 words, I will copy some "lorem ipsum" text into the article. By merely making two changes – adding 300 words or more to the page and modifying the first paragraph to contain the search phrase, we have obtained a green dot and a rating of "Good" in our SEO ranking. With each modification, you should click "Save Draft" to update the SEO status. When you are satisfied with the page layout and SEO, click Publish.

You have optimized the page for one or more specific search strings and are satisfied with the results. Can you immediately go out and search for that phrase in Bing or Google and see your site on the first page? That would be a nice occurrence, but many companies and consultants are seeking that first page for the most sought-after search phrases. Keep making minor changes and you may be able to achieve the "first page golden ranking."

Aside from popularity, should you consider anything else in your search engine optimization efforts? Yes, there is a time frame concern. If you do not utilize all of the tools available, such as the XML sitemap and "ping" of the search engines, it may take weeks for the changes to be discovered. Using these features of the WordPress SEO plugin, the anticipated time frame is reduced from weeks to days, hours or less.

If you have now combined, theoretically, a location and an extremely popular search phrase, your site may appear on the coveted first page. Let's say that you are a book keeper in Raleigh, NC so you create a page mentioning accounting, bookkeeping, books and Raleigh. An hour after publishing the page, you go to Google and search for "bookkeeper Raleigh" and your site shows up as the number 1 selection. Target achieved!

Now let's set this as the home page. On your Dashboard, select the Appearance area and then Customize. Select Static Front Page, choose "A Static Page" and select the page that you have just published. Now all visitors will see this page when they visit your site.

NOTE The process of setting Static Front Page, as shown here, is based on the "spacious" theme. This same process will apply to many themes and provide the desired effect. Some themes have a modified design that loses creativity and functionality when setting the front page into static mode. For example, there is a theme called "Parabola" and it relies heavily on backgrounds and other design features. In order to maintain these User Experience (UX) features, the "static front page" setting is left on "Your latest posts" and the front page displayed by the theme and the front page itself is changed using an option entitled "Parabola Settings." Using this settings page, you can modify the focus from a blog to informative business site.

Your web site is a reflection of your personality and business. You should use it to spread your own views, advertise for your small business and increase the profits in that business. One helpful tool in the achievement of these goals is blog posting. WordPress initially creates a web site designed around blog posts. When writing blog posts for the world to see, you should be concerned with optimizing the posts in order for the world to find them in the search engines. Optimizing blog posts follows the same processes already shown for optimization of web pages..

We have glanced over the detailed subject of search engine optimization. There is a principle to keep in mind when creating SEO-friendly blogs and pages – the statistics and suggestions only apply to the keywords currently selected. If someone chooses to search using a modified keyword string, they can completely miss your site or it may appear much lower than intended. Select your targeted keywords carefully and customize the page or article to cover as many keywords as possible. This chapter covers approximately three hours of time to apply the items discussed. The truth to that is that "the basics" can be covered in three hours. Proper SEO for a single page or blog post can consume many hours all by itself.

SIDE TRIP You have seen how to optimize your page for specific keywords and have been advised that it can take days or weeks for the search engines to find, and reindex, the page changes. Decide on six phrases that directly relate to the focus of your web site. Create three pages of at least 300 words each and incorporate at least two of the phrases multiple times on each page. Use the WordPress SEO suggestions to make these pages rank higher for each of the included search phrases. Ensure that the XML sitemap is enabled along with "ping" of all search engines. After an hour of publishing the pages, search for the chosen phrases and note the results. In an effort to improve the location of your site, you may want to incorporate location and other keywords to narrow the search criteria. While pursuing effective search engine optimization, you may also want to consider social networking posts mentioning your business/products and business listings on sites such as "Google for Business." It is possible to dominate the first search engine pages if you can receive enough social networking posts, testimonials, business listings and other mentions.

When making a measurable and concerted effort to improve search engine ranking, you should change only one thing at a time, and allow at least a day before making another change. This allows a proper amount of time to review the effects of the specific change. Repeat this process of making a single change until you are happy with the performance of your web pages in the search engines.

One thing that we haven't covered so far is having the site available for a select few while it is in development. There are two main areas where this could be a most useful feature - holding off for the final "reveal" while redesigning a site and creating a site which is Ecommerce enabled. Why would Ecommerce enabled matter? You may be working on gathering the final pricing for products and shipping, so you don't want anyone other than your testers to see that the initial price has increased tremendously after all costs have been calculated.

How do we enable maintenance mode to the world, while allowing certain people to have access? Hmmmm … we have already seen that a faulty plugin update can crash our site so that even the administrator can't get in, therefore this is an intriguing question. The answer, of course, is to use a plugin. I have experience with a plugin called "Smart maintenance mode" which allows maintenance mode to be turned on or off, customize the screen displayed and disable maintenance mode for specific roles.

Custom HTML content

```
<p style="text-align:center;"><img
src="http://happycapscreations.com/wp-content/uploads/2014/12
/happycaps-e1417814072298.png" width="40%" height=40%"/></p>
<p style="font-size:x-large;text-align:center;">Happy Caps Creations
will be going live on January 1, 2015</p>
```

This will display Custom HTML content you provide on the Maintenance Mode page

☐ Choose this checkbox to delete the Custom HTML content

Save Settings

Content Preference for Maintenance Mode Page

1. Custom HTML content
2. Countdown
3. Custom Image
4. Custom Heading and Sub Heading
5. Default Heading and Sub Heading

Disable Maintenance Mode for User Roles

Choose the User Roles to see the actual site when the users are logged in with that user role

☑ Administrator ☐ Editor ☐ Author ☐ Contributor ☐ Subscriber

You will notice that this is displayed using Custom HTML Content. In working with this plugin, there is a countdown clock and other features that can be utilized, but they did not seem to integrate well with the custom content which I chose. You will also notice the Administrator role that is being allowed to bypass maintenance mode. Other uses for this functionality may be when you are building up a blog spot and have assigned a group of people to the Editor and Author roles. This plugin could allow access to them while displaying a page similar to the screenshot below for the rest of the world.

Happy Caps Creations will be going live on January 1, 2015

3 MORE WEBSITE SETUP

In our adventure of redesigning a business web site we have registered the domain, created the site and added plugins and pages. So far, we have a nice looking web site. We will make it better, though, by adding many standard web site features to help others find our site and utilize it in an efficient manner.

Return to the dashboard and click Settings. Let's set up some of the options shown below.

Site Title	LinkEmUp Blog
Tagline	Leadership, inspiration, telling your story? We have i *In a few words, explain what this site is about.*
WordPress Address (URL)	http://www.ncwebdesignprogramming.com/wpbl.
Site Address (URL)	http://www.ncwebdesignprogramming.com/wpbl. *Enter the address here if you want your site homepage to be different*
E-mail Address	slink@linkemup.us *This address is used for admin purposes, like new user notification.*
Membership	☑ Anyone can register
New User Default Role	Contributor ▾

Notice that we have set a site title along with a catchy tagline. This information should have been set up during our initial WordPress setup routine, although we can change it here. The email address is important to be able to receive communications generated by our site. Depending on your preferences, you may want to change the default "anyone can register" and user default role. Let's move to the writing options.

SIDE TRIP If you are a sole proprietor in the business, you are the only one who knows the true focus and goals of your business. Call up an associate who may be involved in advertising and discuss a catchy tagline for your business that will draw in customers. You may be able to come up with this in a few hours, or it may take a few weeks to decide on a truly appealing motto. You want something that will be as memorable as "Where's the beef?" and "melts in your mouth, not in your hands." By giving potential customers something to talk about, you will have achieved the most-effective goal - word of mouth advertising.

Default Post Category   Uncategorized ▾

Default Post Format   Standard ▾

Default Link Category   Blogroll ▾

Press This

Press This is a bookmarklet: a little app that runs in your browser and lets you grab bits of the web.

Use Press This to clip text, images and videos from any web page. Then edit and add more straight from Press Th

Drag-and-drop the following link to your bookmarks bar or right click it and add it to your favorites for a posting

✒ Press This

Post via e-mail

To post to WordPress by e-mail you must set up a secret e-mail account with POP3 access. Any mail received at t address very secret. Here are three random strings you could use: `nj01Cy4I` , `0q9y7fHo` , `Ti2BQhGm` .

Mail Server   `mail.example.com`   Port 110

In this screen shot we see the default settings for writing on our site. These are shown mainly to give the options that you have for creating blogs on the site. Rather useful options are the "press this" option and the ability to post via email. How does that work? Excellent question. The users can send an email to a chosen email address, if this option is set up, and that email will be posted as a blog entry. Let's move on to the reading options.

Front page displays
- ⦿ Your latest posts
- ○ A static page (select below)

    Front page: — Select — ▾

    Posts page: — Select — ▾

Blog pages show at most   10 ⇕ posts

Syndication feeds show the most recent   10 ⇕ items

For each article in a feed, show
- ⦿ Full text
- ○ Summary

Search Engine Visibility   ☐ Discourage search engines from indexing this site

It is up to search engines to honor this request.

Since we have added pages to our site, we will be setting this to a static page and select the initial page to be displayed to our web site guests along with the blog page that we will be using. If you want the site to be visible to search engines, be sure to leave the box shown here unchecked. Before checking that box, you should heavily consider the effect – your site will be invisible to the search engines if this box is checked.

The next option, available because we installed the Jetpack plugin, is even more important for site visibility – Publicize.

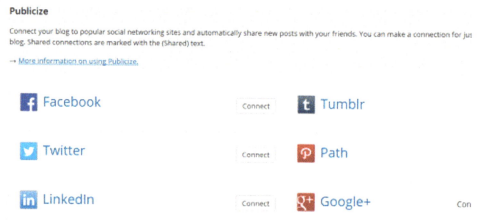

You will use this page of settings to allow posting your blogs to the selected social networks. By using this option, you will be able to type a blog one time and your site will automatically create entries on your connected social networks for you. This will help in building your "social cred" and in the visibility of your communications and web site.

SIDE TRIP You have been introduced to the socialization capabilities provided by the Jetpack plugin. In this list of options are the networks that seem to be the most popular - Facebook, Twitter, LinkedIn and Google+. The good news is that you are not limited to the six networks shown here. You should research the others and decide which plugin will provide the most desirable functionality for your purposes. During this research session, you will find names such as Monarch, Shareaholic and SimpleShare. Previous advice applies regarding conflicts with other plugins, backing up your system before applying new plugins and paying attention to the latest update and version compatibility.

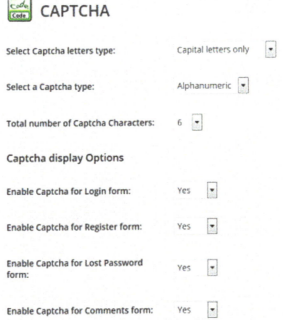

Utilizing a captcha plugin is an excellent idea to enhance the security of users signing up for your site, logging in and posting blogs/comments. This will also ensure that the "bots" are unable to infect your site with unwanted users, posts and comments.

Another thing mentioned previously and not truly expanded on is the concept of registration and sign in to your site. Yes, Virginia, there is a plugin for that. The plugin that has been used in my sites is called "OneAll Social Login" and it is shown below.

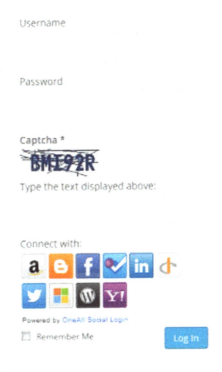

You will notice that the social login is available in addition to the Captcha question so the user gets to choose which method is preferable for login. The social login choices extend well beyond those shown here. Although there are extra setup steps with this plugin, they are well documented and easy to perform. In addition to selecting the social sites used, you will need to set up an API with the OneAll site plus APIs for many of the social sites used.

Is OneAll Social Login too much trouble to set up? After going through the first one, you may believe so. Creating three or four more beyond that will become much easier. Once this functionality is in place and you are able to gather user demographics without requiring additional effort by the user, you will greatly enjoy the value added by this plugin.

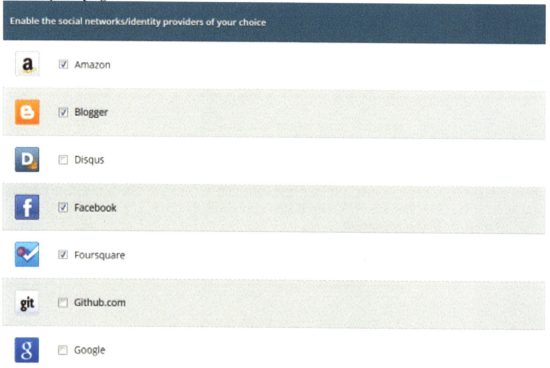

We have covered many useful plugins that can be used to add functionality to your web site. Even though we have seen some additional features enabled through plugins, we have barely "scratched the surface" of what is available for free or a fee.

4 SEARCH ENGINE OPTIMIZATION / SITE VISIBILITY

In the previous chapters, we have successfully covered some of the options available to ensure proper setup and security within your web site. So far, the site is truly functional and quite secure, although we have only given minimal effort to the visibility of our site to search engines and potential visitors. Next we will touch on some specifics for **S**earch **E**ngine **O**ptimization using the Yoast SEO plugin. I call this "just a touch" because proper SEO can take up many pages and many books. By using a plugin, we will be able to better keep up with the regularly changing search provider rules and make your web site more visible to the outside world.

Something that we did not show or address in previous chapters is your permalink settings. Since you may be unfamiliar with a permalink, a little explanation is in order. Permalinks are the way that your page or blog shows up to the search engines and the rest of the world. You could use a structure as generic as "p=123," which uses the post number. Can you see how that would not be helpful for the search engines and potential audience to find your site?

If you take a look at the Settings-Permalinks section of your Dashboard, you will see the following (as of version 4.1)

Permalink Settings

By default WordPress uses web URLs which have question marks and lots of numbers in them; however, WordPress offers structure for your permalinks and archives. This can improve the aesthetics, usability, and forward-compatibility of your lin here are some examples to get you started.

Common Settings

○ Default	http://www.ncwebdesignprogramming.com/wpblog/?p=123	
○ Day and name	http://www.ncwebdesignprogramming.com/wpblog/2015/01/04/sample-post/	
○ Month and name	http://www.ncwebdesignprogramming.com/wpblog/2015/01/sample-post/	
○ Numeric	http://www.ncwebdesignprogramming.com/wpblog/archives/123	
○ Post name	http://www.ncwebdesignprogramming.com/wpblog/sample-post/	
◉ Custom Structure	http://www.ncwebdesignprogramming.com/wpblog	/%category%/%postname%/

You could select from any of these common settings, or create your own structure. Notice that this site has done exactly that, by using category and postname in the permalink. Do you like what we have done so far? Yes, it is impressive, and we haven't gone beyond the basic Wordpress settings.

In researching SEO, you will discover something called "stop words." These are words such as "a," "at" and "the" which should not be used in your search engine titles. Changing your "slug" (or permalink) after the post or page is available to the world is generally not a good idea, because users may have linked to it. Making that change could result in dead links and disgruntled users.

Now we get to work with an excellent plugin for enhancing the SEO of your pages and posts – WordPress SEO by Yoast. Installing this plugin will make suggestions available to enhance the search-ability of both pages and posts. This plugin is the main focus of this final website redesign chapter. Let's start with the end goal, shown below.

Business Web Site Redesign in Eight Hours, Using WordPress – Part 3

In our adventure of redesigning a business web site we have registered the domain.

In this screenshot you get to use the SEO categorization that was introduced in a previous chapter – notice the green dot beside of the SEO label at the top of the screen. This is based on the focus keyword string "business web site redesign." The ranking represented by that green dot considers title, permalink, meta description, content and other factors. Many of these, factors within your control, will be covered in this chapter. Because there are so many search engine optimization factors, covering all of them in detail would take many books. By the time a complete list was compiled, the requirements are likely to have changed.

The most logical starting point is creation of the page or post. Begin design with your target audience in mind. For easier reading, we will focus on a blog post.

What are the reader's interests?

What points of focus would draw the reader into your page or post?

How can you maintain interest in the current content while creating interest in other posts, pages or offerings?

By designing your content with the target reader in mind, you may very well create a masterpiece that "goes viral." Imagine a pyramid with your single, well designed, post at the top. You crafted this with the utmost care and attention to detail. Now it is available for the general public. Not only does it go well with your social friends (hundreds or thousands), but it is a hit with their social networks. In addition to that, the search engines contribute to the growth in popularity because of the many factors that were considered when creating your post.

Enough with the viral fantasizing. You need to know how to turn this fantasy into a reality. Let's begin that adventure now.

You have seen the importance of designing the content appropriately. Use keywords and phrases liberally in the post while keeping the readability level high. What, exactly, does this mean? It means that you should write your post as if it were being graded by your English teacher. Whether this is your fifth, eighth, twelfth or college teacher is determined by the average reading level of your target audience. If you are writing an article on repairing your vehicle, the reading level will be lower than an article on the chemical makeup of spam.

I apologize if this could be considered an insult to auto mechanics. I know a highly educated computer hardware guy with a hobby of rebuilding Corvettes, but he will not be the average reader for any of my articles. This type of person is easy to write for, since he or she will understand most of the vocabulary you use, and will have the desire and capability to research the rest. Your target audience may be easier, or not as easy, to create for.

In addition to focused and informative content, which the search engines will expect, you need to create a truly catchy title and description (see the screenshot below)

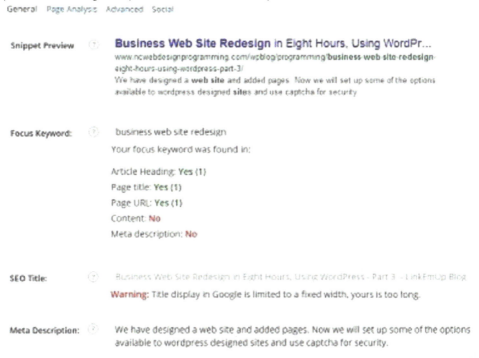

In this screenshot you see all of the settings on the front page of the Yoast SEO plugin and the analysis that produced the "Good" rating previously shown. Although "Good" is the best that you can achieve, Search Engine Optimization can be improved by increasing the number shown beside each of the items. Also keep in mind that this rating is based only on the focus keyword that you have entered. If this is truly the most popular search phrase that your target audience is using, then "you are golden." You could also use this tool to revise the text and other aspects of your post to perform well for other keywords and phrases.

At the bottom of this screenshot, you see two items of utmost importance in search engine optimization - SEO Title and Meta Description. Your SEO title will default to the permalink that is set up, but you should change it to be different, although just as descriptive. In this case, a more descriptive SEO Title may be "WordPress > Business Website Redesign << Effective Plugins."

Another truly helpful piece of the SEO puzzle is the Meta Description. This should contain as many keywords as possible while delivering a readable snippet which will entice the user to click through to your site.

Of course, the target is to see a green dot on all of your posts. That is a utopian target which, for the most part, is unachievable unless you spend an inordinate amount of time crafting your words, paragraphs and entire article. What you will normally see is a mix of "almost there" and "good," as shown below. By the way, this shows four of the 161 articles (as of Sep 2014). Half and half, as displayed here, would not be an unacceptable SEO ranking of articles.

☐	Writing Your Own Book	slink	2014/08/13 Published	Writing Your Own Book - LinkItUp Blog	This article covers some of the details in writing your own book, having it published, and the amount of money that can be made-maybe thousands or millions.	your own book
☐	Business Web Site Redesign in Eight Hours, Using WordPress - Part 3	slink	2014/08/13 Published	Business Web Site Redesign in Eight Hours, Using WordPress - Part 3 LinkItUp Blog	We have designed a web site and added pages. Now we will set up some of the options available to wordpress designed sites and use captcha for security	business web site redesign
☐	Scripture Study Matthew 6 Father Pray Earnestly Model Prayer	slink	2014/08/13 Published	Scripture Study Matthew 6 Father Pray Earnestly Model Prayer - LinkItUp Blog	This Scripture study will cover the Matthew 6 text and the subjects pray in secret, pray earnestly and will close with the model prayer. Read, study, learn.	scripture study matthew 6
☐	Love My Enemies Matthew 5 Bible Study KJV verses 43-48	slink	2014/08/13 Published	Love My Enemies Matthew 5 Bible Study KJV verses 43-48 LinkItUp Blog	This bible study will cover matthew 5 and the subjects prayer for your enemies, being a child of god, loving everyone. We see god's...	matthew 5 bible study

But what about the other three pages of SEO settings? Honestly, I am a programmer by profession, my hobby is being an author and I am still a beginner in search engine optimization. The second tab gives some analysis and suggestions that you can use on individual edits for specific areas of improvement. The third and fourth tabs include some advanced and social settings that I have not really touched, although they can be of great help in improving the appeal of your article to the social networks.

In working with the Yoast SEO plugin, you may have noticed a "Titles" section. This section will give the opportunity to have Yoast create the titles for you. The decision that you have to make would be "is it beneficial to my site?" Even though this is an SEO optimization plugin, there is no viable replacement for the human thought process. If you will invest just a little time and creativity, a manually created title should perform far better than anything that an automation tool can come up with. As the description says, you can override the automatically detected settings if desired (and you know what you are doing).

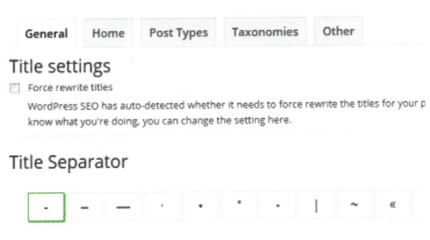

After toggling this checkbox, you should review the settings at the bottom of this page and review/modify the other four tabs in this section. As stated, I believe that the guidance provided by this plugin combined with your thought and creativity will create a much more productive title and meta description.

SIDE TRIP You have been introduced to the Yoast plugin. Their site has many posts and publications available for your research. Take 15 to 30 minutes every few days and do some reading about search engine optimization on the Yoast site and through general web searches. As previously stated, many books have been written on this subject alone and most only "scratched the surface" of effective use of the search engines. This small time commitment will not make you an expert in the subject, but it may lead to more inquisitiveness, curiosity, and extended research into specific topics that you find interesting.

I hope that you have enjoyed these four chapters aimed at redesigning your business web site. As a matter of fact, you may have discovered that you can do all of this in one business day. Although a fully functioning, optimized and popular web site is never finished, the basics can be created in a committed eight hour time frame.

5 EXTENDED FUNCTIONALITY AVAILABLE IN OTHER THEMES

We have mentioned the Parabola theme and the approach utilized in customizing it. We have not addressed any detail of how much functionality is available and how it can be used. This chapter will cover some options in that theme, as an example of the extended functionality available within a customized WordPress theme.

You may be thinking "hmmm ... I have seen a Settings page, but how do I get to these extended settings?" Quite simple, my dear Watson, you will select Appearance and then Parabola Settings from the WordPress Dashboard. Then you will see a screen with the settings shown below (expanded "Layout" option).

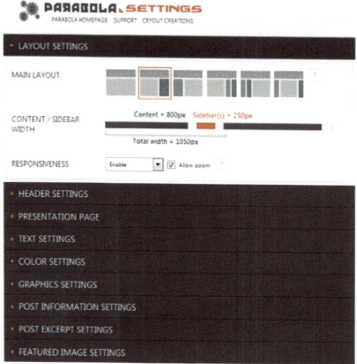

How easy is it to disable the responsiveness of your site? Disable it here with a dropdown. A really big question regards why you would want to do this. I believe there is a viable answer - you want to view the layout on different size screens. You are also able to choose the sidebar layout (or sidebar absence, if desired)

and the default widths of the screen components. You have seen one out of many customization options - let's take a look at the Header section.

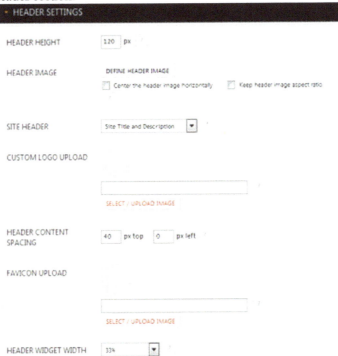

This looks like almost complete control over the header area of your page. You can change the height, image, aspect ratio, logo, spacing and more. In case you are not overwhelmed with the available options (think Maserati versus old VW Bug), we will take a look at the many Presentation Page options next.

When you saw the Parabola theme mentioned in a previous chapter, it was in regards to setting the main page to a Static Front Page. With a standard theme, plus a desire to use a standard page as your main home page, you would select this option. Using that dropdown with the Parabola theme, much of the customized functionality would be lost. One of the most useful features of this theme is a front page slider, which is shown above. As you see by this screenshot, there are many features and behaviors of the slideshow that can be modified.

In addition to the slider, you can choose whether to display the recent posts on the home page. In the case of this site, it is not focused on blogging, so this option is disabled. While we are at it, let's take a look at the options available for the slides within the slideshow.

The title and text will be imposed over the bottom area of the image selected. If the user clicks on the image, the page displayed in the Link section will be loaded. These slide details are relatively standard to any slideshow plugin, although the presence of so many options and features is quite impressive. Not shown in the screenshot are options for extra text to display on the home page and hide some sections on the first page.

A truly useful feature that can make your site unique is the fonts, sizing and spacing used. In a previous chapter, we mentioned that you can customize anything through the CSS settings of your WordPress theme. This is a completely true statement which applies to any WordPress theme that you may select. It is also true that the CSS customization is likely to be lost if you update the theme. By utilizing customizations built into the theme, those changes are retained between upgrades without any special processes.

With all of these options available, you may never have to modify the back-end CSS files in order to make your site appear exactly how you want. Color choices provide another way to make your site stand out from the others. Just like fonts, any colors can be modified through changes to the theme's CSS files. With so many color options available (some shown below), the need to make these back-end modifications should be nearly eradicated.

We have many more options that could be covered in the Parabola theme, but you are left to explore this theme, and any others you may choose, in the following Side Trip.

SIDE TRIP You have seen many of the features used in both basic and enhanced themes. Although we have covered many options and details, it would take this entire book, maybe more, to cover every option available in a single theme. Build on the experience gained from the previous theme-related Side Trip and try out a few of the enhanced themes. Open up your WordPress Dashboard and open Appearance-Themes. Now click on "Add New" and type the word "customizr" in the search box and press ENTER. You will see a theme by that name which has the functionality shown here and well beyond. "Customizable" is the name of another theme that lives up to its name, but it will not be as easy to find. Another theme feature that you may enjoy is full screen width. To view these, select the "Feature Filter" and then check "Full Width Template." To view customizable full-width themes, you may want to check "Theme Options" before clicking on Apply Filters. Two nice looking themes from this selection are called "The Bootstrap" and "Advantage."

As previously stated, you have many theme options available directly from within the WordPress framework. If you do a general web search for WordPress themes, there will be almost 10 million to choose from. Some will be free while others will charge a minimal purchase amount. You will find many WordPress themes priced at $100 or more and some of those can be purchased for exclusive use at a price well beyond that.

The WordPress world is wide open to you. Set a time and dollar budget to be your guide while exploring this world to the extents that these allow. Enjoy your WordPress site while you exercise the customizations shown in the next couple of chapters.

6 CUSTOMIZING YOUR WEB SITE

So far, the web site design that you have created may reflect your own style and preferences, but it has used pre-built plugins to accomplish this. In the next chapter, you will learn how to design functionality and web pages using the PHP programming language. The final chapter will illustrate a custom desktop application written in CSharp which will extend the capabilities of the MarketPress Ecommerce plugin.

Let's start with a little background. The Appalachian Trail spans from Georgia to Maine and covers 2,179 miles as of the creation of this exercise program. You can, of course, start in Maine or Georgia and the mileage can vary depending on the changes that nature throws at us. There are through-hikers who can complete this entire trail in about six months. There are many more who cannot commit to that period of time, or the physical toils, who choose to hike an entire state or local trails. I thank those who have done the hiking and provided the awesome pictures that you will encounter along your exercise journey. The two main sources for the data and pictures are SummitPost for the mileage and Picasa/Flickr/Panoramio (and others) with picture storage.

The entry page at the WalktheAT site looks excellent, with instructions and options after logging in.

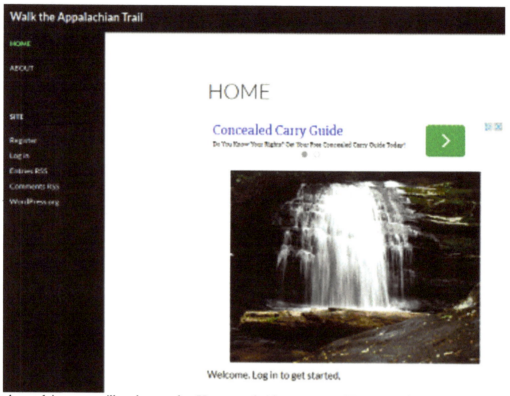

If not logged in, you will only see the Home and About pages. How was the user login requirement functionality achieved? With a plugin, of course. The plugin is named "Nav Menu Roles" by Kathy Darling. In addition to specific roles applied to individual pages, it includes a logged in option.

You may be wondering how hard it could be to restrict access to specific pages. With the "Nav Menu Roles" plugin it is quite simple - select an option. Below we see the menu items (Appearance - Menus) for "View Location" and "My Stats."

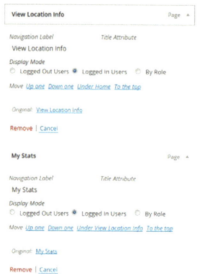

In these two cases, we have selected the option that makes these pages available only to logged in users. We could have just as easily selected users who are logged out or users fitting within specific roles.

SIDE TRIP This is an interesting side trip. The above plugin will keep the menu from displaying if you are not logged in, hence the name "Nav Menu Roles." What it will not do is restrict access to the page through a direct link. In other words, if someone has access to your site with a user ID and you then deactivate that user ID, they will still be able to load the page as long as they have the link saved. The goal of this side trip is to research various plugins and find one that will redirect to the login page if accessing any page while not logged in.

You also see the effect of another plugin used in this page for additional revenue generation - "Adsense Made Easy - Best Simple Ad Inserter." This is tied to your Adsense account and it displays different style ads based on the content of your page. Would you want to annoy your business customers with these ads? I would hope not. In this case, the custom site is a free offering to the public, so the ads are an expected occurrence.

Now that we are logged in, we can go to the View Location Info page.

On this page, selecting the date from a calendar would be a nice feature. In the code, it is looking for your last entry and adding one day. If you exercise every day, or try to, this is a time saving feature.

On this screen, you will notice details about your current location along the Appalachian Trail plus a "View Picture" link. This View Picture link will only be displayed if there is a picture tied to this location. See Appendix C for the code that supports this logic and web page.

A vital part of any useful exercise program is an ability to track your stats. That is available using the "My Stats" link shown above. The initial display is an overall average with an ability to specify a date range to use for stats calculation. The screenshot below shows a selected date range.

```
Overall Totals
Mileage: 2013.60
Time: 587.38 hours
MPH: 3.43
Daily Averages (657)
Mileage: 3.06
Time: 0.89 hours
MPH: 3.43

End date:   2014-12-23

Begin Date:   2014-10-24

    GET STATS

2014-10-24 to 2014-12-23

Weekly Average
Mileage: -13.82
Time: 6.21 hours
MPH: -2.22
Monthly Average
Mileage: -59.23
Time: 26.63 hours
MPH: -2.22
```

Negative mileage - why is that? I am glad that you noticed that detail. This is a screen shot taken from my current mileage and I have completed the trek from GA to ME and the system has turned me around so that I am actually making negative mileage as I head back to Georgia. See Appendix D for the code used to support this logic and web page. By the way, I do nothing extra in entering mileage. It knows that I am on the way back to GA and the system changes my mileage to a negative automatically, while still maintaining a total mileage counter.

Another feature available in this program is the ability to edit the entries that have been made. Suppose that you entered 32 miles when you meant to enter 3.2. Correcting that is not a problem, although it will be a bit disappointing to lose those 28.8 miles in your total mileage count! Of course, the program recalculates the total when you make a change in an entry.

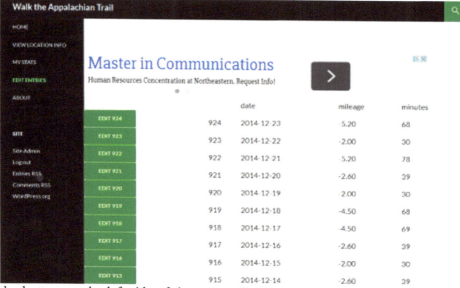

Clicking the button on the left side of the entry will allow you to change the mileage and time in the screen shown below.

This code is displayed and explained in Appendix E and the databases used are shown in Appendix F.

You have seen the functionality that was duplicated from a C# ASP.Net app. It had rather basic functionality, but it worked well for my virtual trip along the Appalachian Trail. A couple of basic functionalities were missing in the original program – the ability to finish one direction and walk back along with tracking time in order to calculate MPH. These have been accommodated with a flag to determine walking direction and an additional database field to track total mileage and current location. Another database field was added to keep track of time taken for each entry. Although these features have been added, you will probably see features that would be nice to have in your own design of this program. Since software and web sites are never truly finished, feel free to add additional desired features and functions. Keep in mind that new code will need to be tested and debugged, since it can affect other areas.

What you haven't seen so far is the exact approach used to create these custom PHP scripts. First, let's assess your logic capabilities. The fact that you are reading this chapter lends credibility to your understanding of logic and commitment to creativity through code.

Even the most thought-out logic has to begin somewhere. WordPress custom logic and screens begin with your theme's base page template - usually named page.php. By following the instructions below, you will make a copy of this file and rename it to whatever you want. This example has three custom pages which were covered above - viewloc.php, stats.php and editentry.php.

Access your website file manager (or open your web directories in an FTP program such as Filezilla)

Locate page.php, which should be located in the wp-content/themes/<your theme>/page-templates directory

Copy and rename page.php to whatever filename(s) you will be using for your custom page

Within your WordPress Dashboard, go to Appearance-Editor

In the right side listing, you will see the filename(s) just copied. Be sure to pay attention to the filename itself, instead of the description.

Edit Entry Page Page
Template
(page-templates/editentry.php)

Full Width Page Page
Template
(page-templates/full-width.php)

Stats Page Page Template
(page-templates/stats.php)

View Location Page Page
Template
(page-templates/viewloc.php)

Click on the desired file, edit and save

In order to change the description displayed above the filename, you should change the "Template Name" in the commented section at the top of the page.

When editing the file, be sure to replace only the code between the "<?php" and "?>" tags within the "content-area" div.

Back up any files before making changes so that you can get back to the original if things should go completely wrong.

It may take a few tries to find the exact location and produce the explicit user experience that you are seeking, be patient and persistent.

SIDE TRIP You may be able to use a WordPress plugin such as "File Away" for file copying functionality. Remember, though, that you have a programmer mentality. Therefore, you are not afraid to get "down and dirty" with the back end files of your web site. If you take this side trip, take a look at file copy/file rename plugins which will allow you to work with the back-end WordPress files. Be sure to focus on system, or back-end, files. You will find many plugins for copying posts and pages.

After editing, these will appear as regular pages which will be named based on the "Template Name" assigned in the comment section of the code. Appendices C, D and E will illustrate this concept in combination with the code used to create these pages and the logic behind them. You can select the page name to be assigned to your menu structure when ready, using the Appearance-Menus selection from your WordPress Dashboard.

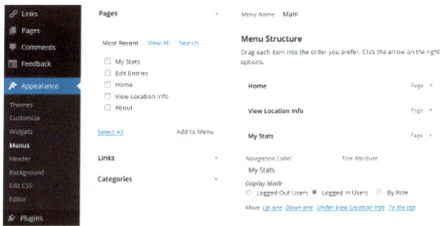

You have already seen a similar menu screenshot that focuses on the fact that this is only displayed in the menu for logged in users. This shows you that the menus can be assigned from within the Appearance section of your WordPress Dashboard. Assign a page to the menu by checking the box beside it and clicking on "Add to Menu."

After adding, you can move the item up or down and also indent to the level desired. After clicking the "Save Menu" button (upper right, not shown), it is available for all of your site visitors.

If creating your own custom PHP page, this approach works great. What if you want to download and import these files? In that case, you won't have to worry about copying and renaming. Just upload to the correct directory of your web site, and you are ready to add to the menu. The main thing to keep in mind with that approach is that the files you are downloading were designed around the Twenty Fourteen theme. If you are using a different theme, you should create new pages with the copy/rename method shown above and then copy the PHP code from the downloaded files into them.

You should also be aware that some plugins will modify the page.php file. An excellent example is the AdSense plugin. If you use a customized page from someone else's site, you may include extraneous code which will not fit well into your theme.

7 ADDING DESKTOP BASED FUNCTIONALITY

Let's set up a scenario. You have a need to integrate Ecommerce functionality into your web site. The research has been done and the decision has been made about the best plugin to fit your needs. You have now set up the plugin and connected it to your selected payment method. It works beautifully, at least from the standpoint of accepting payment and shipping the product.

Your product is a bit unique, though, in that respect. The customer pays in full, receives a box and ships the raw material back to you. Your company takes the raw material and produces the final product to ship to the customer. This is not the standard Ecommerce product flow, and the creator of the plugin says that it does not accommodate customization to this degree. Their software does not offer the modification but they offer a customized solution, at a cost.

You have already put time into searching for the perfect Ecommerce fit, and more time into getting it set up and operational. You don't want to spend even more money for enhancing Ecommerce functionality that has not yet produced a single dollar in revenue. You start thinking, "I can do programming work in PHP to customize a web site, maybe I can create a CSharp program to provide the capabilities that I need" so you propose this idea to your boss.

A discussion follows regarding the "time is money" fact but you are able to convince the boss that this is a function that can be used elsewhere once created for this specific purpose. The boss thinks that you are crazy to believe that it can be done in such a short time, but you are allowed 20 working hours to create a desktop-based program using C#.

There is a Billy Joel song that says, "You may be right, I may be crazy." You are out to prove that you are not crazy. The goal is to create your own custom program that can be modified and used in other areas instead of paying for a focused, single-use, program created by a third party. The gauntlet has been thrown down and you are ready for the task. Read on to complete that challenge and move forth as the victor.

FUNCTIONALITY DESIRED

Retrieve the last 60 days or orders from the web site and display them in read only grid. That grid displays order date, number and status.

Click on an item in that grid to display the customer email address, name, address, city state zip, phone, order number, status and items in the order.

Statuses are: Paid, Box Shipped, In Progress, Shipped and Closed.

To reproduce the Ecommerce functionality, an email will be sent to the customer when the status changes.

The only modifiable item in this program is order status. In order to avoid changing the web site database, you need to incorporate a local database containing order number and status.

NOTE This C# program was written using Visual Studio 2010 and uses .Net Framework 4. The version of .Net will be dependent on the version of MySQL Connector that you utilize - 6.4.4.0 in this case. The function of this program is to connect a WordPress database hosted on GoDaddy with the MarketPress Lite plugin installed for Ecommerce functionality. Your host may require a different approach for direct access to the database and another Ecommerce program will use a different database and/or fields to store the order information. At the end of this chapter, you will find a link to download the code. Keep in mind that the code is not operational as written since the login information for the data links has been cleansed.

Let's start with the design of the local SQLCe database.

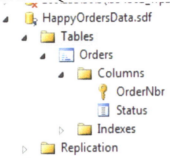

As stated above, there are only two fields needed - OrderNbr (primary key) and Status. As you will see later in the actual code, the approach is to attempt to find the order number and then either update or create depending on the results of the search.

The program itself looks like

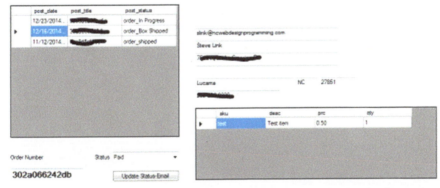

You may be thinking "How do we manage all of this detail using only the database shown above?" The simple answer is that we use the Ecommerce fields inside of the WordPress database in read-only mode to load all of the order information. We then look up the order number and modify what is displayed based on the status saved in the local database. Of course, any personal information has been cleansed from this display.

Enough with the visual demonstration, let's get into the design and the code! You can see from the screen above that there are two grids, nine text boxes, two labels, a combo box and a button. All of the processing happens in four functions - initial form load, row click in left grid, button click and a function to determine the IP address of the current user. We will start with the IP address function.

```
public string GetPublicIP()
{
//This routine uses the checkip.dynds.org site to return the outside IP address
// This code was found in a MS Forum and is unmodified from that source
String direction = "";
WebRequest request = WebRequest.Create("http://checkip.dyndns.org/");
using (WebResponse response = request.GetResponse())
using (StreamReader stream = new StreamReader(response.GetResponseStream()))
{
```

```
direction = stream.ReadToEnd();
}
//Search for the ip in the html
int first = direction.IndexOf("Address: ") + 9;
int last = direction.LastIndexOf("</body>");
direction = direction.Substring(first, last - first);
return direction;
}
```

Why do we need to get the outside IP address? In the case of GoDaddy, there is a security feature that will only allow specific IP addresses to access their databases. This function may not be required by your web host.

Now we get to see how it is utilized - in the Form_Load function.

```
private void Form1_Load(object sender, EventArgs e)
{
MySqlConnection connstr = new MySqlConnection();
try
{
connstr.ConnectionString = "server=*****;User Id=*****;password=*****;Persist Security Info=True;database=*****";
connstr.Open();
string stdt = DateTime.Now.ToString("yyyy-MM-dd");
MySqlCommand cmd = new MySqlCommand("select post_date,post_title,post_status,post_content from wp_posts where post_type = 'mp_order' and post_date>=SUBDATE('" + stdt + "',60) order by post_date desc", connstr);
MySqlDataAdapter da = new MySqlDataAdapter(cmd); // connstr.CreateCommand()
DataTable dt = new DataTable();
da.Fill(dt);
SqlCeConnection localconn = new SqlCeConnection();
try
{
string localcs = @"C:\*****\*****OrdersData.sdf";
localconn.ConnectionString = "Data Source=" + localcs + ";Persist Security Info = False;";
localconn.Open();
}
catch (Exception exception)
{
MessageBox.Show(exception.ToString());
}
SqlCeCommand cmd2 = new SqlCeCommand("select * from orders where OrderNbr = '" + txtOrdNbr.Text + "'", localconn);
SqlCeDataAdapter da2 = new SqlCeDataAdapter(cmd2);
DataTable dt2 = new DataTable();
foreach (DataRow row in dt.Rows)
{
cmd2.CommandText = "select * from orders where OrderNbr = '" + row[1] + "'";
da2.Fill(dt2);
if (dt2.Rows.Count > 0)
{
row[2] = dt2.Rows[0].ItemArray[1].ToString();
}
dt2.Rows.Clear();
}
```

```
dgvDisplay.DataSource = dt;
dgvDisplay.Columns[3].Visible = false;
dgvDisplay.Columns[2].Width = 110;
dgvDisplay.Columns[1].Width = 110;
dgvDisplay.Columns[0].Width = 75;
dgvDisplay.ClearSelection();
}
catch (Exception exception)
{
string myip = GetPublicIP();
MessageBox.Show("Your IP address is: " + myip + "\nYour web site database security is
blocking access top your database\nStep 1 - Log into GoDaddy with your ***** Login name
and password\nStep 2 - Launch *****.com web site\nStep 3 - Under the Database section
below, click 'Remote MySQL'\nStep 4 - Add the IP address shown to the left and click Add
Host\nYou can now log out of GoDaddy and should be able to load the orders from your web
site.");
}
}
```

Let's start at the top of this code and work our way to the end. First, we are setting up the MySQL database code within a Try … Catch block so that the processing will fall through to the error processing if there is a failure in loading the database. Next, we set up the current date and load all entries for the past sixty days - in this case, we need only the post_date,post_title, post_status and post_content for the data with a post_type of "mp_order." We are sorting that in descending date order and use it to fill a data table.

Next, we open the local SQLCe database within a Try … Catch block and load it into a data table. After loading the order information into the display textboxes and grid, we get to the Catch statement which calls the GetPublicIP() routine and displays an error message detailing how to log in and grant access to your web databases. Now we get to the fun part of parsing out the order details after selecting an order from the left grid.

```
private void dgvDisplay_CellClick(object sender, DataGridViewCellEventArgs e)
{
int selrow = e.RowIndex;
textBox1.Text = dgvDisplay.Rows[selrow].Cells[3].Value.ToString();
string ordnbr = dgvDisplay.Rows[selrow].Cells[1].Value.ToString();
string stat = dgvDisplay.Rows[selrow].Cells[2].Value.ToString().Substring(6);
string[] items = null;
DataTable orditems = new DataTable();
orditems.Columns.Add("sku");
orditems.Columns.Add("desc");
orditems.Columns.Add("prc");
orditems.Columns.Add("qty");
string datastr = textBox1.Text,item="",sku,desc,prc,qty;
int nextloc = 0,nextsku=1,startloc=0,custloc=0;
// cycle through string until not SKU
while (nextsku == 1)
{
nextloc = datastr.IndexOf("{s:3", custloc + 4);
if (nextloc > -1)
{
item = datastr.Substring(nextloc + 1, datastr.IndexOf("}",nextloc) - nextloc);
nextloc = item.Length+1;
custloc += nextloc;
items = item.Split(';');
```

```
    sku = items[1].Substring(items[1].IndexOf("\"") + 1, items[1].LastIndexOf("\"") -
items[1].IndexOf("\"") - 1);
    desc = items[3].Substring(items[3].IndexOf("\"") + 1, items[3].LastIndexOf("\"") -
items[3].IndexOf("\"") - 1);
    prc = items[7].Substring(items[7].IndexOf("\"") + 1, items[7].LastIndexOf("\"") -
items[7].IndexOf("\"") - 1);
    qty = items[9].Substring(items[9].IndexOf(":") + 1);
    orditems.Rows.Add(sku, desc, prc, qty);
    nextloc += startloc;
    }
    else
    {
    nextsku = 0;
    }
    }
    dgvItems.DataSource = orditems;
    custloc = datastr.IndexOf("{s:5");
    string cust = datastr.Substring(custloc + 1);
    string[] custinfo = cust.Split(';');
    txtOrdNbr.Text = ordnbr;
    cboStatus.Text = stat;
    txtEmail.Text = custinfo[1].Substring(custinfo[1].IndexOf("\"") + 1,
custinfo[1].LastIndexOf("\"") - custinfo[1].IndexOf("\"") - 1);
    txtName.Text = custinfo[3].Substring(custinfo[3].IndexOf("\"") + 1,
custinfo[3].LastIndexOf("\"") - custinfo[3].IndexOf("\"") - 1);
    txtAddr1.Text = custinfo[5].Substring(custinfo[5].IndexOf("\"") + 1,
custinfo[5].LastIndexOf("\"") - custinfo[5].IndexOf("\"") - 1);
    txtAddr2.Text = custinfo[7].Substring(custinfo[7].IndexOf("\"") + 1,
custinfo[7].LastIndexOf("\"") - custinfo[7].IndexOf("\"") - 1);
    txtCity.Text = custinfo[9].Substring(custinfo[9].IndexOf("\"") + 1,
custinfo[9].LastIndexOf("\"") - custinfo[9].IndexOf("\"") - 1);
    txtSt.Text = custinfo[11].Substring(custinfo[11].IndexOf("\"") + 1,
custinfo[11].LastIndexOf("\"") - custinfo[11].IndexOf("\"") - 1);
    txtZip.Text = custinfo[13].Substring(custinfo[13].IndexOf("\"") + 1,
custinfo[13].LastIndexOf("\"") - custinfo[13].IndexOf("\"") - 1);
    txtPhone.Text = custinfo[17].Substring(custinfo[17].IndexOf("\"") + 1,
custinfo[17].LastIndexOf("\"") - custinfo[17].IndexOf("\"") - 1);
    }
```

As you can tell by the name, this is triggered when the user clicks on a row of the grid containing the orders. First, we determine the row that was clicked on, so that details for the selected order can be loaded. Then we populate the text boxes with the loaded data and create a datatable to use for loading the individual item details.

As the comment says, the next block of code loads an ordered item and puts it in the right grid. It then checks to see if another order exists and loads it. Finally, after all orders have been loaded into the data table, the grid is populated with the contents of that data table.

Finally, we load all of the customer information and display it on screen. There can be one or more items ordered, but only one customer information record. As we have already seen, this is a rather simple program with only one more section of code - the button click. We will look at that one now.

In the requirements, we have a need to save the status for use in later program sessions. This is in addition to emailing the customer once the order status changes. In a business situation, you will generally know the software in use. Your business may use Exchange and/or the user may have Outlook installed as the mail client. In this case, since we don't know the email client, we use straight SMTP to send the email. Although there are various publicly available SMTP servers, we choose to use our own business host. Take a look at the code below.

```
private void btnUpdate_Click(object sender, EventArgs e)
{
// does this order number exist in local db? If so, update status, if not add with
current status
SqlCeConnection localconn = new SqlCeConnection();
try
{
string localcs = @"C:\*****\*****Data.sdf";
localconn.ConnectionString = "Data Source="+ localcs +";Persist Security Info =
False;";
localconn.Open();
}
catch (Exception exception)
{
MessageBox.Show(exception.ToString());
}
SqlCeCommand cmd = new SqlCeCommand("select * from orders where OrderNbr = '" +
txtOrdNbr.Text + "'",localconn);
SqlCeDataAdapter da = new SqlCeDataAdapter(cmd);
DataTable dt = new DataTable();
da.Fill(dt);
if (dt.Rows.Count > 0)
{
cmd.CommandText = "update orders set Status = 'order_" + cboStatus.SelectedItem + "'
where OrderNbr = '" + txtOrdNbr.Text + "'";
cmd.ExecuteNonQuery();
}
else
{
cmd.CommandText = "insert into orders (OrderNbr,Status) values ('" + txtOrdNbr.Text +
"','order_" + cboStatus.SelectedItem + "')";
cmd.ExecuteNonQuery();
}
// Now send the email notifying the customer that the order status has changed
string custemail = txtEmail.Text.Trim();
string emsubj = "Your Order Number " + txtOrdNbr.Text.Trim() + " from Happy Caps
Creations";
string embody = "";
if (cboStatus.SelectedItem.ToString() == "Box Shipped")
{
embody = "We thank you for your order. This email is a notification that the status
has changed to '" + cboStatus.SelectedItem + "' and a postage-paid box has been shipped
to you. Once it has been received, simply follow the enclosed instructions to return your
cap(s) to us.\n\*****\nOrder Fulfillment department";
}
else
{
embody = "We thank you for you order. This email is a notification that the status has
changed to '" + cboStatus.SelectedItem + "'.\nYour cap(s) have been received and your
custom sports creation is under way. We take pride in providing excellent value in the
product(s) that you have ordered and memorable customer support throughout the entire
process. We are hard at work on completing your custom sports creation.\n\*****\nOrder
```

```
Fulfillment department";
    }
    MailMessage msg = new MailMessage("orders@*****", custemail);
    SmtpClient emailhost = new SmtpClient();
    try
    {
    emailhost.Port = 25;
    emailhost.DeliveryMethod = SmtpDeliveryMethod.Network;
    emailhost.UseDefaultCredentials = false;
    emailhost.Host = "mail.*****";
    emailhost.Credentials = new NetworkCredential("orders@*****", "*****");
    msg.Subject = emsubj;
    msg.Body = embody;
    emailhost.Send(msg);
    MessageBox.Show("Status updated, email sent");
    }
    catch (Exception exception)
    {
    MessageBox.Show(exception.ToString());
    }
    }
```

Although not advised, we are using port 25, which is the unsecured (non-SSL) port. We could set useSSL to true and use a different port, if desired. Port 25 is the usual unsecure port and it should apply to most accounts. The secured port and requirements can vary by host.

Did you take this as an excellent learning opportunity by creating the C# project and typing in all of the code? If so, that is a quite impressive feat and I am sure that you learned plenty to apply in your job or business. You may prefer to download the code and, instead, learn from making small changes. In that case, you can download from http://www.ncwebdesignprogramming.com/bookfiles/wordpress4Orders.zip.

APPENDIX A: DISABLING PLUGINS ON GODADDY HOSTING ACCOUNT

Unless you are extremely careful with backups and updates, there will eventually be a need for recovery of a site that is stuck in maintenance mode due to applied updates. The biggest culprit in this problem, to me at least, seems to be the JetPack plugin. A JetPack update has caused an unusable site at least twice in a six month period.

The first time this happens, it can truly cause a panic since you can't get into the dashboard to fix the problem. If you call the web host, the first question they will ask is "do you have backups?" If you can answer YES to that, restore from them and all is well. A NO answer to that question, depending on the support policy of your web host, may result in an immediate "sorry, can't help you" answer. I can say that they tried to help at GoDaddy, but then resorted to that answer since they did not create the problem and were unable to resolve it.

Thanks to a slight modification of the results found through am internet search, there is a rather simple answer - for GoDaddy, and any other hosts using CPanel. Access your database and disable the plugins. This will bring the site back up and then you can re-enable the plugins, one at a time if necessary, and attempt the problem update again. See the steps below for a step-by-step guide on disabling the plugins on a GoDaddy hosted WordPress site.

Log into your database using phpMyAdmin, or whatever admin program is needed to connect to your database.

Browse the wp_options table and find the active_plugins record.

You will see a list of the plugins in the format of
i:1;s:19:"akismet/akismet.php";

Copy the text for the plugin that you were updating to Notepad and then remove that text.

Save the record back to the database.

As noted above, you are now able to access the site and dashboard. You can either enable all other plugins or do them one at a time to be sure of no conflicts. You should also take the precaution of backing up your site, either through your web host's control panel (most recoverable) or through a plugin in WordPress, before adding new plugins that may conflict with one or more already installed.

As the well-known statement goes, "that was easy" and there was no need to panic.

APPENDIX B: WALKTHEAT EXERCISE PROGRAM IN ACTION

We have presented this program as an excellent addition to your company's exercise and wellness plan. Feel free to modify it in any way for your own personal or corporate use.

The program can be viewed and used, free of charge, at http://walktheat.ncwebdesignprogramming.com.

NOTE All rights to this code are reserved by the original creator - LinkEmUp - in regards to any commercial distribution of this code or concept. Special thanks to those who are committed to the maintenance of the Appalachian Trail along with those who have hiked the trail in order to provide the excellent scenery displayed in this program. Thanks, also, to the web hosts providing storage and availability of these excellent pictures

APPENDIX C: PHP CODE AND SCREEN FOR APPALACHIAN TRAIL ENTRY

The code below can be typed in as a learning experience or you can download it from
http://www.ncwebdesignprogramming.com/bookfiles/wordpress4AppendixC.zip.

```php
<?php
/**
 * This is a custom template designed for viewing the current location
 * Template Name: View Location Page
 *
 * @package WordPress
 * @subpackage Twenty_Fourteen
 * @since Twenty Fourteen 1.0
 */

get_header(); ?>
<?php

?>
<script type="text/javascript">
function popnbr()
{
alert('loaded');
}
function hello(nbr)
{
alert(nbr);
}
function setCookie(cname, cvalue, exdays) {
var d = new Date();
d.setTime(d.getTime() + (exdays*60*1000));
var expires = "expires="+d.toUTCString();
document.cookie = cname + "=" + cvalue + "; " + expires;
}
function getCookie(cname) {
var name = cname + "=";
var ca = document.cookie.split(';');
for(var i=0; i<ca.length; i++) {
var c = ca[i];
```

```
while (c.charAt(0)==' ') c = c.substring(1);
if (c.indexOf(name) != -1) return c.substring(name.length, c.length);
}
return "";
}
function checkCookie() {
var user = getCookie("username");
if (user != "") {
alert("Welcome again " + user);
} else {
user = prompt("Please enter your name:", "");
if (user != "" && user != null) {
setCookie("username", user, 365);
}
}
}
</script>

<div id="main-content" class="main-content">
<?php
if ( is_front_page() && twentyfourteen_has_featured_posts() ) {
// Include the featured content template.
get_template_part( 'featured-content' );
}
?>
<div id="primary" class="content-area">
<div id="content" class="site-content" role="main">
<script async src="//pagead2.googlesyndication.com/pagead/js/adsbygoogle.js"></script>
<!-- WalktheAT -->
<ins class="adsbygoogle"  style="display:inline-block;width:728px;height:90px"
 data-ad-client="*****" data-ad-slot="*****"></ins>
<script>
(adsbygoogle = window.adsbygoogle || []).push({});
</script>
<?php
get_currentuserinfo();
$curruser = $current_user->user_login;
$added = 0;
global $wpdb;
// *** curruser comparison below required to loop only once
if (!empty($_GET['act']) && $curruser != '') {
echo "<font color='red'><b>Entry added</b></font><br><br>";
$dt = $_GET['inpdt'];
$mlg = $_GET['inpmiles'];
$dir = $_GET['dir'];
$tim = $_GET['inptime'];
if($dir=='R')
{
$mlg = $_GET['inpmiles'] * -1;
}
$locs2 = $wpdb->get_results("SELECT * FROM AEntries where Username = '$curruser' order
by dateent desc limit 1;");
  foreach($locs2 as $loc2){
$mlg2 = $loc2->currttl+$mlg;
```

48

```
$mlg3 = $loc2->currloc+$mlg;
if($dir=='R')
{
$mlg3 = $loc2->currloc+($mlg*-1);
}
if($mlg2>=2178.3)
{
echo "<font color='blue'><b>Congratulations, you have reached Baxter Peak in Maine,
have a nice trip back to Springer Mt, GA</b></font><br><br>";
$mlg2 = 2178.3;
// flip direction to R in ALogins
$wpdb->query($wpdb->prepare("update ALogins set dir = 'R' where Username =
'$curruser'"));
}
if($mlg2<=0)
{
echo "<font color='blue'><b>Welcome to Springer Mt, GA, have a nice trip to Baxter
Peak in Maine</b></font><br><br>";
$mlg2 = 0;
// flip direction to F in ALogins
$wpdb->query($wpdb->prepare("update ALogins set dir = 'F' where Username =
'$curruser'"));
}
$currdt = $loc2->dateent;
}
$wpdb->query($wpdb->prepare("insert into AEntries
(Username,dateent,entry,currttl,currloc,minwalked) values
('%s','%s','%s','%s','%s','%s')", array($curruser,$dt,$mlg,$mlg2,$mlg3,$tim)));
}
// need to check ALogins for existence of $curruser
// If not, create and set Username = $curruser and dir to 'F'
$exists = "";
$dist = "F";
$locs3 = $wpdb->get_results("SELECT * FROM ALogins where Username = '$curruser';");
foreach($locs3 as $loc3){
$exists = $loc3->Username;
$dist = $loc3->dir;
}
if($exists==="")
{
$wpdb->query($wpdb->prepare("insert into ALogins (Username,dir) values ('%s','%s')",
array($curruser,'F')));
}
$locs = $wpdb->get_results("SELECT * FROM AEntries where Username = '$curruser' order
by dateent desc limit 1;");
foreach($locs as $loc){
$miles = $loc->currttl;
$totmiles = $loc->currloc;
$currdt = $loc->dateent;
}
$currlocs = $wpdb->get_results("SELECT * FROM AMileage where Distance >= $miles limit
1;");
foreach($currlocs as $currloc){
echo "<br>Mileage: ".$miles."<br>";
```

```php
echo "Location: ".$currloc->Feature."<br>";
echo "Elevation: ".$currloc->Elevation."<br>";
echo "County/State: ".$currloc->County."/".$currloc->State."<br>";
echo "Long/Lat: ".$currloc->Long."/".$currloc->Lat."<br>";
echo "Total Mileage: ".$totmiles."<br><br>";
if ($currloc->Picture <> "")
echo "<a href=".$currloc->Picture.">View Picture</a>";
}
?>
$newcurr = date("Y-m-d",strtotime("+1 day",strtotime($currdt)));
echo "<form action='index.php' method='get'>";
echo "<input type='hidden' name='act' value='run'>";
echo "<input type='hidden' name='dir' value='$dist'>";
printf("Date entered: <input type='text' name='inpdt' value='%s'><br>",$newcurr);
printf("Add mileage: <input type='text' name='inpmiles'><br>");
printf("How many minutes? <input type='text' name='inptime'><br>");
echo "<input type='submit' value='Insert Entry'>";
echo "</form>";
?>
<script async src="//pagead2.googlesyndication.com/pagead/js/adsbygoogle.js"></script>
<!-- WalktheAT -->
<ins class="adsbygoogle" style="display:inline-block;width:728px;height:90px"
data-ad-client="*****" data-ad-slot="*****"></ins>
<script>
(adsbygoogle = window.adsbygoogle || []).push({});
</script>
</div><!-- #content -->
</div><!-- #primary -->
<?php get_sidebar( 'content' ); ?>
</div><!-- #main-content -->
<?php
get_sidebar();
get_footer();
```

APPENDIX D: PHP CODE FOR SCREEN AND LOGIC IN APPALACHIAN TRAIL MY STATS

The code below can be typed in as a learning experience or you can download it from http://www.ncwebdesignprogramming.com/bookfiles/wordpress4AppendixD.zip.

```php
<?php
/**
 * This is a custom template designed for viewing the current location
 * Template Name: Stats Page
 *
 * @package WordPress
 * @subpackage Twenty_Fourteen
 * @since Twenty Fourteen 1.0
 *
 * This will display total mileage, time, and miles per hour
 * plus average daily total, time,miles per hour
 * There will also be a date range selection which will populate
 * Weekly average total, time, miles per hour (if greater than 14 days)
 * Monthly average total, time, miles per hour (if greater than 60 days)
 */

get_header(); ?>
<?php
?>
<div id="main-content" class="main-content">
<?php
if ( is_front_page() && twentyfourteen_has_featured_posts() ) {
// Include the featured content template.
//get_template_part( 'featured-content' );
}
?>
<div id="primary" class="content-area">
<div id="content" class="site-content" role="main">
<script async src="//pagead2.googlesyndication.com/pagead/js/adsbygoogle.js"></script>
<!-- WalktheAT -->
<ins class="adsbygoogle"  style="display:inline-block;width:728px;height:90px"
data-ad-client="*****" data-ad-slot="*****"></ins>
<script>
```

```php
(adsbygoogle = window.adsbygoogle || []).push({});
</script>
<?php
get_currentuserinfo();
$curruser = $current_user->user_login;
global $wpdb;
// need to check ALogins for existence of $curruser
// If not, create and set Username = $curruser and dir to 'F'
$exists = "";
$dist = "F";
$locs3 = $wpdb->get_results("SELECT * FROM ALogins where Username = '$curruser';");
foreach($locs3 as $loc3){
$exists = $loc3->Username;
$dist = $loc3->dir;
}
if($exists===""")
{
$wpdb->query($wpdb->prepare("insert into ALogins (Username,dir) values ('%s','%s')",
array($curruser,'F')));
}
$locs = $wpdb->get_results("SELECT * FROM AEntries where Username = '$curruser' order
by dateent desc limit 1;");
foreach($locs as $loc){
$miles = $loc->currttl;
}
$locs11 = $wpdb->get_results("SELECT sum(minwalked) as ttlmins FROM AEntries where
Username = '$curruser';");
foreach($locs11 as $loc11){
$time = $loc11->ttlmins;
}
$locs12 = $wpdb->get_results("SELECT count(minwalked) as ttldays FROM AEntries where
Username = '$curruser';");
foreach($locs12 as $loc12){
$days = $loc12->ttldays;
}
echo "<br><B>Overall Totals</B><br>";
echo "Mileage: ".$miles."<br>";
echo "Time: ".(round(($time/60),2))." hours<br>";
echo "MPH: ".(round(($miles/($time/60)),2))."<br>";
echo "<B>Daily Averages</B> (".$days.")<br>";
echo "Mileage: ".(round(($miles/$days),2))."<br>";
echo "Time: ".(round((($time/60)/$days),2))." hours<br>";
echo "MPH: ".(round(($miles/($time/60)),2))."<br>";
$date =time () ;
//This puts the day, month, and year in separate variables
$day = date('d', $date) ;
$month = date('m', $date) ;
$year = date('Y', $date) ;
$currdt = $month . "/" . $day . "/" . $year;
$newcurr = date("Y-m-d",strtotime("-1 day",strtotime($currdt)));
$lastcurr = date("Y-m-d",strtotime("-61 day",strtotime($currdt)));
echo "<form action='index.php' method='get'>";
echo "<input type='hidden' name='act' value='run'>";
printf("End date: <input type='text' name='endt' value='%s'><br>",$newcurr);
```

```
printf("Begin Date: <input type='text' name='begdt' value='%s'><br>",$lastcurr);
echo "<input type='submit' value='Get Stats'>";
echo "</form>";
if (!empty($_GET['act'])) {
$dt1 = $_GET['endt'];
$dt2 = $_GET['begdt'];
$dt3 = date_create($dt1);
$dt4 = date_create($dt2);
$dt5 = $dt3->diff($dt4)->days;
$nbrmth = $dt5/30;
$nbrweek = $dt5/7;
$locs2 = $wpdb->get_results("SELECT sum(entry) as ttlmiles FROM AEntries where
Username = '$curruser' and dateent >= '$dt2' and dateent <= '$dt1';");
  foreach($locs2 as $loc2){
$ttlmlg = $loc2->ttlmiles;
}
$locs3 = $wpdb->get_results("SELECT sum(minwalked) as ttlmins FROM AEntries where
Username = '$curruser' and dateent >= '$dt2' and dateent <= '$dt1';");
  foreach($locs3 as $loc3){
$ttltime = $loc3->ttlmins;
}
$locs4 = $wpdb->get_results("SELECT count(minwalked) as ttldays FROM AEntries where
Username = '$curruser' and dateent >= '$dt2' and dateent <= '$dt1';");
  foreach($locs4 as $loc4){
$ttlday = $loc4->ttldays;
}
if($nbrweek>=2){
echo "<br>".$dt2." to ".$dt1."<br><br>";
echo "<B>Weekly Average</B><br>";
echo "Mileage: ".(round(($ttlmlg/$nbrweek),2))."<br>";
echo "Time: ".(round(($ttltime/60/$nbrweek),2))." hours<br>";
echo "MPH: ".(round(($ttlmlg/($ttltime/60)),2))."<br>";
}
if($nbrmth>=2){
echo "<B>Monthly Average</B><br>";
echo "Mileage: ".(round(($ttlmlg/$nbrmth),2))."<br>";
echo "Time: ".(round(($ttltime/60/$nbrmth),2))." hours<br>";
echo "MPH: ".(round(($ttlmlg/($ttltime/60)),2))."<br>";
}}
?>
<script async src="//pagead2.googlesyndication.com/pagead/js/adsbygoogle.js"></script>
<!-- WalktheAT -->
<ins class="adsbygoogle" style="display:inline-block;width:728px;height:90px"
data-ad-client="*****" data-ad-slot="*****"></ins>
<script>
(adsbygoogle = window.adsbygoogle || []).push({});
</script>
</div><!-- #content -->
</div><!-- #primary -->
<?php get_sidebar( 'content' ); ?>
</div><!-- #main-content -->
<?php
get_sidebar();
get_footer();
```

APPENDIX E: PHP CODE AND LOGIC USED IN APPALACHIAN TRAIL EDIT ENTRIES

The code below can be typed in as a learning experience or you can download it from http://www.ncwebdesignprogramming.com/bookfiles/wordpress4AppendixE.zip.

```php
<?php
/**
 * This is a custom template designed for editing the entries
 * Template Name: Edit Entry Page
 *
 * @package WordPress
 * @subpackage Twenty_Fourteen
 * @since Twenty Fourteen 1.0
 */

get_header(); ?>
<?php

?>
<div id="main-content" class="main-content">
<?php
if ( is_front_page() && twentyfourteen_has_featured_posts() ) {
// Include the featured content template.
get_template_part( 'featured-content' );
}
?>
<div id="primary" class="content-area">
<div id="content" class="site-content" role="main">
<script async src="//pagead2.googlesyndication.com/pagead/js/adsbygoogle.js"></script>
<!-- WalktheAT -->
<ins class="adsbygoogle" style="display:inline-block;width:728px;height:90px"
data-ad-client="*****" data-ad-slot="*****"></ins>
<script>
(adsbygoogle = window.adsbygoogle || []).push({});
</script>
<?php
get_currentuserinfo();
$curruser = $current_user->user_login;
```

```
global $wpdb;
if (!empty($_GET['act'])) {
$btn = substr($_GET['submit'],5);
$loceds = $wpdb->get_results("SELECT * FROM AEntries where id = $btn;");
unset($act);
echo "<form action='index.php' method='get'>";
echo "<input type='hidden' name='id2' value='$btn'>";
echo "<input type='hidden' name='act2' value='run'>";
foreach($loceds as $loced){
printf("%s Entry ",$loced->dateent);
printf("<input type='text' name='entry2' value='%s'>  ",$loced->entry);
printf("<input type='text' name='min2' value='%s'><br>",$loced->minwalked);
printf("<input type='submit' name='submit2' value='Save Change'>");
}
echo "</form>";
}
if (!empty($_GET['act2'])) {
//echo "place saving code here";
$id3 = $_GET['id2'];
$mlg3 = $_GET['entry2'];
$min3 = $_GET['min2'];
//if F, need to verify mileage positive, R = negative mileage
$dist = "F";
$locs3 = $wpdb->get_results("SELECT * FROM ALogins where Username = '$curruser';");
foreach($locs3 as $loc3){
$exists = $loc3->Username;
$dist = $loc3->dir;
}
if($dist=='R')
{
if($mlg3>0)
{
$mlg3 = $mlg3*-1;
}
}
if($dist=='F')
{
if($mlg3<0)
{
$mlg3 = $mlg3*-1;
}
echo "<font color='red'><b>Update saved</b></font><br><br>";
$wpdb->query($wpdb->prepare("update AEntries set entry = $mlg3, minwalked = $min3
where id = $id3"));
$ttls = $wpdb->get_results("select sum(entry) ttlmlg from AEntries where Username =
'$curruser' ");
foreach($ttls as $ttl){
$currttl3 = $ttl->ttlmlg;
}
$wpdb->query($wpdb->prepare("update AEntries set currttl = $currttl3 where Username =
'$curruser' "));
// sum abs() to determine total mileage
$ttls = $wpdb->get_results("select sum(abs(entry)) ttlmlg from AEntries where Username
= '$curruser' ");
```

```
foreach($ttls as $ttl){
$currttl3 = $ttl->ttlmlg;
}
$wpdb->query($wpdb->prepare("update AEntries set currloc = $currttl3 where Username =
'$curruser' "));
unset($act2);
}
// put table here for editing the entries
$locs = $wpdb->get_results("SELECT * FROM AEntries where Username = '$curruser' order
by dateent desc;");
echo "<form action='index.php' method='get'>";
echo "<input type='hidden' name='act' value='run'>";
echo "<table>";
echo "<tr><td></td><td></td>";
echo "<td>date</td>";
echo "<td>mileage</td>";
echo "<td>minutes</td>";
echo "</tr>";
foreach($locs as $loc){
echo "<tr>";
echo "<td><input type='submit' name='submit' value='Edit $loc->id'></td>";
echo "<td>".$loc->id."</td>";
echo "<td>".$loc->dateent."</td>";
echo "<td>".$loc->entry."</td>";
echo "<td>".$loc->minwalked."</td>";
echo "</tr>";
}
echo "</table>";
echo "</form>";
?>
<script async src="//pagead2.googlesyndication.com/pagead/js/adsbygoogle.js"></script>
<!-- WalktheAT -->
<ins class="adsbygoogle" style="display:inline-block;width:728px;height:90px"
data-ad-client="*****" data-ad-slot="*****"></ins>
<script>
(adsbygoogle = window.adsbygoogle || []).push({});
</script>
</div><!-- #content -->
</div><!-- #primary -->
<?php get_sidebar( 'content' ); ?>
</div><!-- #main-content -->
<?php
get_sidebar();
get_footer();
```

APPENDIX F: DATABASES USED FOR THE CUSTOMIZATIONS

Below you have a screenshot of the database structure used to support the exercise tracking functionality. These tables are available for download at

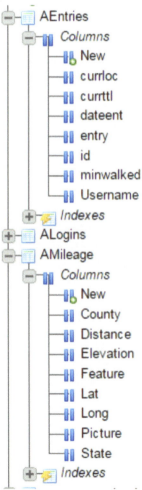

These will be imported into your WordPress database and accessed by the PHP code included in these appendices. The field types and other specifics for the AEntries table are

	#	Name	Type	Collation	Attributes	Null	Default	Extra
☐	1	**id**	bigint(15)			No	*None*	AUTO_INCREMENT
☐	2	**Username**	varchar(10)	utf8_general_ci		No	*None*	
☐	3	**dateent**	date			No	*None*	
☐	4	**entry**	decimal(5,2)			No	*None*	
☐	5	**currttl**	decimal(10,2)			No	*None*	
☐	6	**currloc**	decimal(10,2)			Yes	*NULL*	
☐	7	**minwalked**	int(11)			Yes	*NULL*	

The AMileage table is set up as

	#	Name	Type	Collation	Attributes	Null	Default	Extra
☐	1	**Distance**	decimal(10,2)			No	*None*	
☐	2	**Feature**	varchar(75)	utf8_general_ci		No	*None*	
☐	3	**Elevation**	smallint(4)			Yes	*NULL*	
☐	4	**State**	varchar(2)	utf8_general_ci		Yes	*NULL*	
☐	5	**County**	varchar(20)	utf8_general_ci		Yes	*NULL*	
☐	6	**Long**	decimal(10,4)			Yes	*NULL*	
☐	7	**Lat**	decimal(10,4)			Yes	*NULL*	
☐	8	**Picture**	varchar(150)	utf8_general_ci		Yes	*NULL*	

In order to use and test this functionality, you should create the AEntries table (shown above) in your current WordPress database using your MySQL database maintenance environment. The AMileage table is rather large and will be sued for reporting current location information and pictures. It can be downloaded at http://www.ncwebdesignprogramming.com/bookfiles/wordpress4AMileage.zip. This unzips to a .sql file and you should import it into your current WordPress database.

NOTE You have seen quite a bit of discussion about "your current WordPress database" and "MySQL database maintenance environment." Due to the variations in web hosts and their plans, I can't be more specific than that. I can tell you that on my GoDaddy hosting plan, I have multiple WordPress sites within a single database and they are named similar to "xxx_wp1," "xxx_wp2" and I am using MyPHPAdmin to access my databases and tables. There are other hosting options available with GoDaddy, which are likely to use different naming conventions and your web host may use completely different naming styles. Your host's support desk should be able to help in these discoveries.

The fields used for the order tracking program are not custom fields, at least not for the MarketPress Lite Ecommerce plugin that was used. That plugin uses the standard wp_posts table and the fields post_date, post_content, post_title, post_status and post_type seem the most important.

If you select another Ecommerce plugin, it will likely use different tables and fields. You should now feel confident enough to modify the included CSharp code to add additional power to desktop-based order management.

ABOUT THE AUTHOR

Stephen J. Link is a "computer guy" by profession, an author by hobby, and a Layman in the study of God's Word. He has a computer support book entitled "Link Em Up On Outlook" that was published in 2004 as a paperback (renamed to "Power Outlook" in reprint). He also has over 125 articles covering various topics published on his own blog and independent sites. Various Books have been published covering a number of topics. As a programmer, he has a unique approach to help you master the ability to create the code for automating processes and adding efficiency to your client's or employer's processes.

OTHER WORKS BY STEPHEN LINK AND LINK EM UP, PUBLISHING DIVISION

Programming and Design

HTML5, CSS3, Javascript and JQuery Mobile Programming: Beginning to End Cross-Platform App Design
Complete, Responsive, Mobile App Design Using Visual Studio: Integrating MySQL Database into your web page
Four Programming Languages Creating a Complete Webscraper Application
Excel Programming through VBA: A Complete Macro Driven Excel 2010 Application

Christian Study

Volume 1 of the Potter's Clay series: Mold Your Spirit with a Study in Proverbs
Volume 2 of the Potter's Clay series: Mold Your Spirit with a Study in Matthew
Volume 3 of the Potter's Clay series: Mold Your Spirit with a Study in John
Volume 4 of the Potter's Clay series: Mold Your Spirit with another Study in John
Volume 5 of the Potter's Clay series: Mold Your Spirit with a Study in Hebrews
Volume 6 of the Potter's Clay series: Mold Your Spirit with a Study in Acts

Your Computer

Control Your Windows 7 View: Use a Single Wallpaper Across All of Your Screens

Your Money

Making the Most of Your Money in a Recovering Economy

Most are in Ebook format and are available across multiple platforms. You can start at
http://publishing.ncwebdesignprogramming.com to select the book and platform needed. As time allows, these books will be made available for purchase in print.

www.ingramcontent.com/pod-product-compliance
Lightning Source LLC
Chambersburg PA
CBHW041431050326
40690CB00002B/499

9 781508 610250